MAMMALS

Text by Sarah Lovett

John Muir Publications
Santa Fe, New Mexico

Special thanks to:
• Kent Newton, Curator of Mammals, Albuquerque Zoo
• Bonnie Jacobs, Primate Consultant
• Bat Conservation International

John Muir Publications, P.O. Box 613, Santa Fe, New Mexico 87504
Copyright © 1993 by John Muir Publications
All rights reserved. Published 1996
Printed in the United States of America

Second edition. First printing August 1996

Library of Congress Cataloging-in-Publication Data
Lovett, Sarah, 1953–
    Mammals / text by Sarah Lovett; [illustrations,
Mary Sundstrom, Beth Evans]. — 2nd ed.
        p.   cm. — (Extremely weird)
    Includes index.
    Summary: Describes several unusual mammals,
including the Tasmanian devil, three-toed sloth, anteater,
and musk-ox.
    ISBN 1-56261-284-0 (pbk.)
    1. Mammals—Miscellanea—Juvenile literature.
    [1. Mammals.] I. Sundstrom, Mary, ill.
    II. Evans, Beth, ill.   III. Title. IV. Series:
    Lovett, Sarah, 1953–
    Extremely weird.
QL706.2.L66   1996
599 — dc20   96-14771
                                           CIP
                                            AC

Extremely Weird Logo Art: Peter Aschwanden
Illustrations: Mary Sundstrom, Beth Evans
Design: Sally Blakemore
Printer: Guynes Lithographers

Distributed to the book trade by
Publishers Group West
Emeryville, California

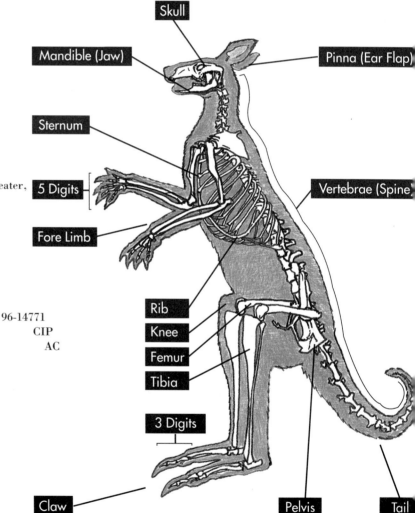

Cover photo: SLENDER-TAILED MEERKAT (*Suricata suricatta*)
Sunbathing and perching like prairie dogs are favorite activities of slender-tailed
meerkats. These very social mammals live in colonies of ten to 15 individuals.
Meerkats live in Africa, and they eat insects, small vertebrates, eggs, and some
greenery. Meerkats use more than ten vocal sounds, including a threat growl and
an alarm bark, to communicate.
Cover photo courtesy Animals Animals © David MacDonald

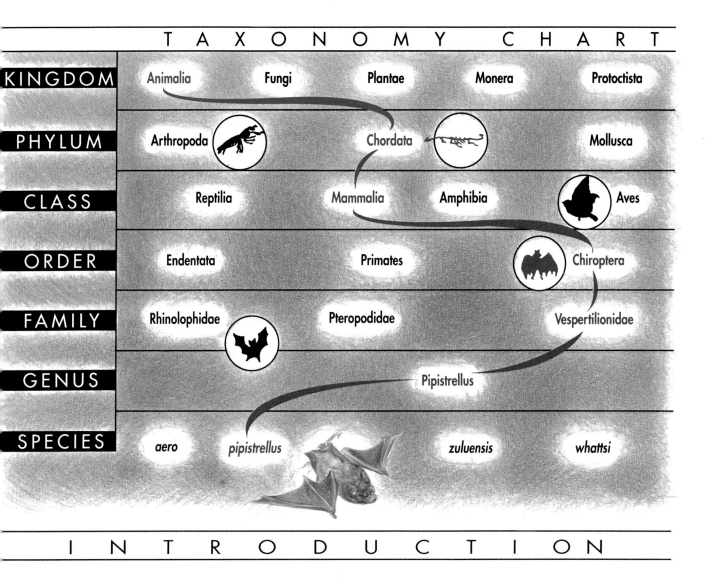

KINGDOM	Animalia	Fungi	Plantae	Monera	Protoctista
PHYLUM	Arthropoda	Chordata		Mollusca
CLASS	Reptilia	Mammalia	Amphibia	Aves
ORDER	Endentata	Primates	Chiroptera
FAMILY	Rhinolophidae	Pteropodidae	Vespertilionidae
GENUS		Pipistrellus	
SPECIES	aero	*pipistrellus*	zuluensis	whattsi

I N T R O D U C T I O N

What do the thimble-sized bumblebee bat and the 170-ton blue whale have in common? If you guessed they both belong to the scientific order *Mammalia*, you're right. They're both mammals.

Mammals—including us humans—are the only animals that breathe air and nurse their young, have hinged backbones, hair, and a four-chambered heart, *and* maintain a constant internal body temperature. (This means mammals are *homoiothermic*. Reptiles and amphibians, in contrast, depend on their outside environment for body heat.) Most mammals give birth to live young, but a few—echidnas and platypuses, for instance—are egg-laying.

Out of roughly 1 million known animal species on the planet, about 4,300 species are mammals. This may sound like a lot, but compare it with 20,000 species of fishes or 100,000 species of insects. So mammals belong to a very small (but important) club. Without other mammals, humans would probably not survive, and we'd certainly be overwhelmed by legions of insects.

To keep track of the millions of animal and plant species on Earth, scientists use a universal system called taxonomy. Taxonomy starts with the five main groups of all living things, the kingdoms, and then divides those into the next group down—phylum, then class, order, family, genus, and, finally, species. Members of a species look similar and can reproduce with each other.

For an example of how taxonomy works, follow the highlighted lines above to see how the pipistrelle bat, *Pipistrellus pipistrellus*, is classified. In this book, the scientific name of each animal is listed next to the common name. The first word is the genus. The second word is the species.

Turn to the glossarized index at the back of this book if you're looking for a specific animal, or for special information (what's a proboscis, for instance), or for the definition of a word you don't understand.

TASMANIAN DEVIL (*Sarcophilus harrisii*)

MARY SUNDSTROM

Sporting blackish-brown fur, white patches on its rump, and a pink snout, ears, feet, and tail, the Tasmanian devil might be mistaken for a tiny bear. This pouched mammal moves slowly, even clumsily. It is a predator—not a very skilled one, though—and a nifty scavenger. The Tasmanian devil feeds mainly on rabbits, wombats, wallabies, and sheep, mostly as carrion (the flesh of dead animals). (It also eats poisonous snakes!) It is equipped with a strong jaw and bone-crushing teeth, the better to eat fur and bones. To find its food, the Tasmanian devil depends on a keen sense of smell and may sniff the ground like a dog. Although this critter prefers solid ground, it is able to climb trees.

Tasmanian devils are active at night. By day they prefer to hide out in grassy, leafy burrows or inside hollow logs and caves. They also seem to enjoy sunbathing.

The Tasmanian devil lives only in Tasmania. Long ago, its range probably included much of Australia, but that was before the dingo, a wild dog, was introduced Down Under and competed with the Tasmanian devil for food.

Although the Tasmanian devil has a reputation for a devilish temper, some scientists say those tantrums are exaggerated. Nevertheless, Tasmanian devils are definitely aggressive with each other.

The Tasmanian devil once scavenged the remains of animals killed by the great Tasmanian wolf, a carnivore that is now extinct.

BETH EVANS

MAMMALS

STAR-NOSED MOLE (Condylura cristata)

Is it a starfish on four legs? A space monster? A mutant ninja rodent? Well, actually, it's a star-nosed mole. This critter boasts 22 extremely weird fleshy rays (tentacles) that sprout from its muzzle. Its eyes are small, its ears barely show, and its tail is scaly and sparsely haired. Each spring, the star-nosed mole's tail increases to the size of a #2 pencil; the extra fat provides energy during the mating season.

Star-nosed moles live in North America all the way from Manitoba, Canada, south to Georgia. They measure about 15 to 20 centimeters (6 to 8 inches) from head to tip of tail.

Star-nosed moles are expert swimmers and divers. They use all four feet to paddle, and they can even cruise under ice in winter. Their dense blackish-brown fur acts like a wet suit and is partly water repellent. Star-nosed moles collect food—aquatic insects, crustaceans, and small fishes—on the bottom of ponds and streams. To grab a bite, all but the star-nosed mole's top two nose tentacles are constantly in motion.

Of course, star-nosed moles can eat on land, too. A favorite meal is lots of juicy earthworms. For this reason, some gardeners and farmers consider them pests.

Star-nosed moles live in small colonies, and within each family group, the male and female winter together. In the spring, the female gives birth to a litter of from two to seven young. These youngsters seem independent at the age of three weeks. Could you imagine having to earn a living at that age?

Did anyone ever tell you, "Don't make a mountain out of a molehill?" Star-nosed moles live in burrows underground. They prefer muddy soil, and when they unearth tunnels, molehills are formed. Star-nosed moles usually stay underground during the day and come out at night.

MAMMALS

PROBOSCIS MONKEY *(Nasalis larvatus)*

If the nose knows, then a male proboscis monkey knows all because his nose just doesn't stop growing. In fact, it may reach a length of 10 centimeters (about 4 inches)—so long, it overhangs his mouth. To female monkeys, the longer the male's nose, the stronger the sex appeal.

With such a long schnozz, is it any wonder the proboscis monkey kee-honks when it is happily devouring shoots, leaves, and assorted fruits? To snooze, adults stretch out on their backs while their young swing from grown-ups' tails or squeeze the biggest nose that's handy.

Proboscis monkeys love to get into the swim. They high-dive 15 meters (about 50 feet) from trees, swim under water, and then dogpaddle across streams, lakes, and even in oceans. Waterlogged proboscis monkeys have been rescued far from ocean shores by fishing boats.

Proboscis monkeys may grow to a height of 76 centimeters ($2\frac{1}{2}$ feet not counting their tail), and they may weigh as much as 22 kilograms (about 50 pounds). They live in very flexible social groups.

Although the button-eyed male proboscis monkeys are famous for their heroic noses and pinkish-brown faces, their young are born with deep blue faces and tiny noses.

Proboscis monkeys get their name from a Latin word for an elephant's trunk. Their noses are fleshy and flexible, and some are so long they get in the way when these animals drink or eat.

The nose of the male proboscis monkey keeps growing, and growing, and growing its whole life. Because females prefer to mate with the longest-nosed males, evolution ensures that proboscis monkeys will remain the Cyranos of the rain forest.

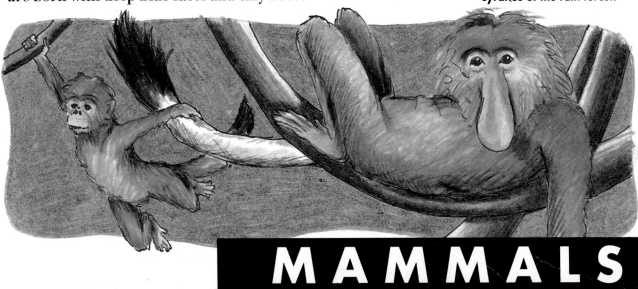

MAMMALS

THREE-TOED SLOTH *(Bradypus tridactylus)*

Hanging out is nothing unusual for the three-toed sloth. In fact, this critter spends most of its life in trees hanging from limbs or sitting in branch forks in the forests of southern Venezuela, the Guianas, and northern Brazil.

The three-toed sloth stays in one tree—especially the cecropia—for long periods. It carefully picks tender leaves, twigs, and buds to eat.

These sloths do come down to the ground but only once or twice a week. When they are grounded, they urinate and defecate and then move to the next tree. Because their terrestrial form of locomotion is a slow crawl, they risk attack by predators. They use their sharp claws to defend themselves and also to climb and to grasp food.

Most of the time, three-toed sloths move extremely slooooowly. For this reason, they depend on a swivel neck so they can be on the lookout for enemies. One or two extra neck vertebrae (bones) gives them 270-degree turning power—about three-quarters of a circle. Compare that to your own ability to twist your neck 180 degrees or so—half a circle.

Because many of the trees are being cut down where three-toed sloths live, they are endangered by loss of habitat.

Young three-toed sloths are carried on their mother's abdomen for months until they feed on their own.

The three-toed sloth has gray-ish-brown fur and brown speckles on its shoulders. If this sloth appears to be green, that's because algae sometimes grows on its coat.

MAMMALS

Smooth as Silk

SILKY ANTEATER *(Cyclopes didactylus)*

The silky anteater may devour between 700 and 5,000 ants (count 'em) per night depending on its size, age, and sex. Its long, tacky, wormlike tongue is made to stick to ants, termites, and some other insects.

Silky anteaters live in tropical forests from southern Mexico to Bolivia and Brazil. By day, they rest in shady spots under leaves and vines; by night, they go to work. Treetops are great places to find insects and termites, and silk-cotton treetops are best of all. That's because these trees have seed pods that are soft and silvery and provide excellent camouflage.

While silky anteaters prey on creepy crawlies, harpy eagles and owls prey on silky anteaters. To defend themselves, silky anteaters raise up on their hind legs, grasp tree branches with their feet, wrap their prehensile (grasping) tails around twigs, and extend the claws on their forefeet. Unfortunately, this threat posture doesn't always offer much protection.

Silky anteaters are named for their soft, silky golden hair. They sport pink noses, black eyes, reddish feet, and sharp, curved claws on their second and third fingers.

Silky anteaters make a tree-hole nest of dry leaves for their young. The single off-spring is raised by both parents, who feed it partially digested insects.

The National Wildlife Federation is the nation's largest conservation organization. For more than fifty years, NWF has worked to conserve wildlife and its habitat. NWF was instrumental in obtaining enactment of the Endangered Species Act in 1973 and has continued working to defend and strengthen that important environmental law. Write: NWF, 1400 16th Street, N.W., Washington, D.C. 20036.

MAMMALS

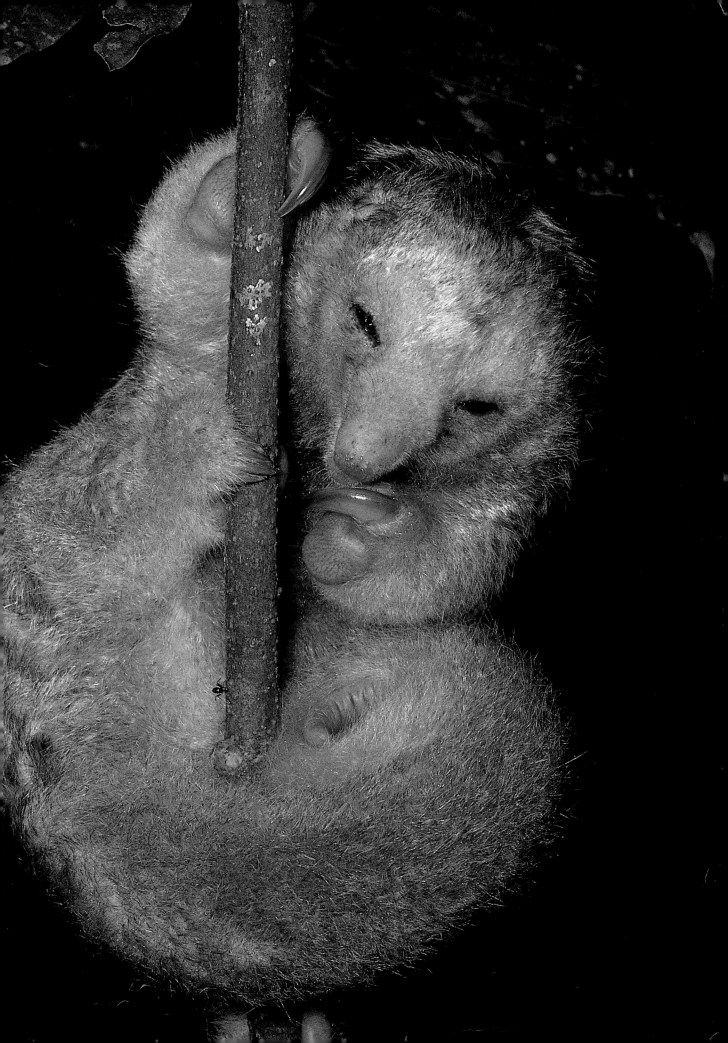

PIPISTRELLE BAT *(Pipistrellus pipistrellus)*

Lots of mammals can jump, trot, skip, and swim, but bats are the only mammals that can fly. In fact, some can reach an airspeed of more than 96 kilometers (60 miles) per hour and an altitude of more than 3 kilometers (10,000 feet). Not every kind of bat can do that. Since there are more than 900 bat species worldwide, it's not surprising that each has its own specialized abilities. Some bats devour insects by the pound, others dine solely on fruit, and still others prefer frogs, birds, and even blood!

Bats vary in size from the largest, the flying fox, which has a wingspan of more than 152 centimeters (5 feet), to the most minuscule, the bumblebee bat, which is only 12 centimeters (5 inches) across with wings outstretched and weighs less than a dime.

Bats are extremely important in the balance of nature. Because they pollinate, reseed, and help control insect populations, you might call them nature's gardeners.

The pipistrelle bat lives in Europe, Algeria, Libya, and Morocco. It is an insectivorous bat, which is a long way of saying it dines on insects. Like most bats, the pipistrelle flies out of its roost at dusk and hunts almost all night long. By day, it roosts in trees, caves, or even under the eaves of buildings.

Dracula, vampire, ghost, demon! Because bats hunt at night in complete darkness, superstitious people have long feared their "supernatural" powers. As we learn more about the world, bats have revealed their non-aggressive nature, and their "supernatural" powers have turned out to be extremely natural!

Bat Conservation International (BCI) can give you more information on bats. This nonprofit organization funds worldwide bat education and conservation projects. They also publish *BATS*, a newsletter for members of all ages. For a donation of any size, you can receive easy-to-follow bat house plans. Write to BCI at P.O. Box 162603, Austin, TX 78716.

MAMMALS

SPOTTED HYENA *(Crocuta crocuta)*

Spotted hyenas boast jaws that may be the most powerful for their size of any living mammal. That's all the better for devouring entire carcasses—skin *and* bones—of wildebeests, zebras, and other prey. In fact, each spotted hyena can devour 14.5 kilograms (about 31 pounds!) of food per meal.

Although they are able hunters (often running in packs of 10 to 25 members), spotted hyenas also scavenge for carrion, which makes them part of nature's recycling project.

A spotted hyena sports black-brown spots on its coarse, yellowish fur. The female is larger than the male, and that's important because she is also the leader of the pack.

Spotted hyenas live on the open plains and rocky lowlands of Africa south of the Sahara Desert. They spend their days in deserted aardvark holes or natural cave dens. At twilight they emerge to begin the night's work. On the hunt, spotted hyenas average 40 to 50 kilometers per hour (about 30 mph), although their maximum speed is 60 kilometers per hour (37 mph).

Some humans consider the hyena beneficial because it is a scavenger. For other humans, the hyena is viewed with superstitious fear. Some tribes put their dead out for hyenas to eat.

The "laughing" hyena gives its famous spine-tingling laugh when it's being chased or attacked.

MAMMALS

SNUB-NOSED MONKEY *(Rhinopithecus roxellana)*

Monkeys are primates that can be divided into two large groups: Old World and New World. New World monkeys live in South and Central America. Some have prehensile tails that can reach and grab like a third arm. None have tough "sitting pads" on their rear ends like Old World monkeys.

Old World monkeys live in Africa, Southeast Asia, and the Malay Archipelago. They have tough pads (like calluses) on their rumps so they can sleep sitting up in trees.

Snub-nosed monkeys, who live in the high mountain forests of China, belong to the Old World group. They spend most of their time in trees—and head straight for the high branches when frightened—but they do come down to the ground to feed and socialize.

Tender fir and pine needles as well as bamboo shoots, fruits, buds, and leaves are all part of the snub-nosed monkey's diet. Food isn't always easy to find, because this monkey lives in snowy weather at least half the year.

Although snub-nosed monkeys are known to travel in troops of 100 to 600 individuals, there are probably smaller groups of four to six adults and their young within each troop.

When snub-nosed monkeys happen on a good source of food, they say it loud: "Ga-ga!"

Captive primates can be more aggressive than their relatives in the wild. That's because they are forced to live in small spaces and compete for food. Human primates in big cities are usually more aggressive and grumpy than their country cousins.

In the Middle Ages, physicians dissected the bodies of monkeys so they could learn more about human anatomy. In those days, dissecting a human body for medical purposes was strictly against the rules.

MAMMALS

Tappin' Tapir

BAIRD'S TAPIR (*Tapirus bairdii*)

Ungulates are mammals that have hooves. Odd-toed ungulates come in a variety of sizes, shapes, and colors. What they have in common is the hard, bony hoof at the end of their legs and their toe count—an odd number. Rhinoceroses, horses, and tapirs are all odd-toed mammals. They look very different, but they are related.

Baird's tapir sports a brown coat that fits right in—with its surroundings, that is. This animal is dark reddish-brown on top and usually lighter below. Its shady coloring provides camouflage in the forests of southern Mexico, Colombia, and Ecuador.

Tapirs live in the lowlands where they are able to find lots of water. They like to wallow in shallow rivers, and that may help them shake off mites, ticks, and other parasites.

Fossil remains prove that tapirs haven't changed much for many millions of years. All four species still have a short trunk of a nose (and a keen sense of smell). They have four toes on their front feet and three toes on the back. Tapirs can grow to a weight of 226 kilograms (500 pounds) and a length of 250 centimeters (about 8 feet).

Shy, docile tapirs are nocturnal critters: they sleep the day away and do their "work" at night.

Tapirs are nifty runners, waders, sliders, divers, and swimmers. Their shape allows them to move quickly through underbrush.

MAMMALS

NAKED MOLE-RAT (*Heterocephalus glaber*)

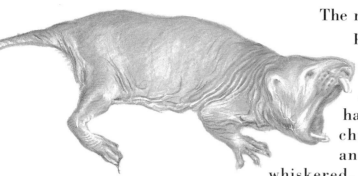

The mole-rat's wrinkled pinkish-yellowish skin looks naked at first glance. Look again: a few pale hairs sprout from its chunky head, body and tail, its lips are whiskered, and its feet are fringed. The hairs on the naked mole-rat's feet act as tiny brooms that collect and sweep away loose dirt during digging.

Naked mole rats are adapted to the dirty life. Colonies of twenty to thirty members build nifty burrow systems underground. One system can stretch for 300 meters (almost 1,000 feet!) and includes a community nest chamber as well as many entrances and exits and rooms for emergencies.

To dig their tunnels, mole-rats form a relay line. The rat at the earth's surface loosens the soil and kicks it backward to the next rat in line, who kicks it to the next, and so on. When enough dirt is collected deep in the tunnel, the inside rat backs its way to the surface. As it moves out—and the others move up—it pushes earth with its hind feet. One by one, the mole-rats push out the earth. If you happened upon a naked mole-rat burrow construction site, you'd see dirt flying in all directions.

Naked mole-rats are found in Ethiopia, Somalia, and Kenya.

A female naked mole-rat always leads the colony while younger naked mole-rats act as workers.

Of all mammals, naked mole-rats have the hardest time maintaining a constant internal body temperature. To avoid exhaustion, they only construct or remodel their burrows during the early mornings and late afternoons when the temperature is moderate.

MAMMALS

HAIRY ARMADILLO *(Chaetophractus villosus)*

Armored in a double layer of horn and bone, the hairy armadillo looks as weird as other armadillos—only hairier. How does the hairy armadillo develop its armor? A baby armadillo is born with tough, leathery skin that hardens into horny plates or bands as it grows. This armored shell is very handy for hiding from other animals. And because the plates are surrounded by flexible skin, armadillos of some species can roll up into a ball when threatened. That's good protection for an armadillo's belly, which is covered with soft skin and hair instead of scales.

Adult hairy armadillos may measure as much as 57 centimeters (about 2 feet) from head to tail's end and weigh as much as 2 kilograms (4½ pounds). They live in open areas of northern Paraguay and parts of Bolivia and Argentina.

Hairy armadillos burrow under dead animals to munch on maggots and other insects. They also kill small snakes by hurling themselves on the reptile's body and cutting it with the edges of their armor.

The tongue of the giant armadillo—a relative of the hairy armadillo—is shaped like a worm, and it has many small bumps covered with sticky saliva. These sticky bumps are great for catching ants, worms, spiders, and insects. But the giant armadillo's favorite food treat is a mouthful of termites. Because giant armadillos have claws and powerful limbs, they are very good diggers and scratchers. They can tear up termite hills in search of food and leave holes so big a human can fit inside.

MAMMALS

RED KANGAROO (*Macropus rufus*)

Kangaroos, wallabies, opossums, and bandicoots are members of the scientific order *Marsupialia*; they're commonly called marsupials. Marsupials are different from all other mammals because they have special features of reproduction. Most female marsupials have an abdominal (belly) pouch in which they carry their young. Some species of marsupials develop a pouch only during reproduction, and some pouches are just an extra fold of skin. After marsupial young are born, they crawl into their mother's pouch where they nurse—for weeks or even months!—before emerging.

Giant red kangaroos are the biggest marsupials in the world. They may measure 280 centimeters (about 9 feet) from their head to the tip of their tail and weigh almost 90 kilograms (200 pounds). They live on the grass-covered plains of Australia, and like all kangaroos, they are herbivores (plant-eaters).

Red kangaroos live in organized groups called "mobs." A mob usually consists of two to ten individuals, but many mobs may gather at the same water hole during dry seasons.

The red kangaroo depends on its strong hindquarters to keep it leaping and hopping. Its tail acts as a rudder for balance during leaps, and it makes a third leg for sitting. The tail is so strong, it can support the red kangaroo's entire weight. Indeed, when they move slowly, kangaroos use a "five-footed" gait: they balance on their forearms and tail as they swing their hind legs forward. At high speed, kangaroos can leap 9 meters (29 feet) or more.

Within one day after a young red kangaroo leaves its mother's pouch, another baby may be born.

The red kangaroo is the world's largest marsupial; still, a red kangaroo newborn weighs less than one gram (.035 ounce) at birth.

All species of kangaroos are most active at twilight or at night. They often feed from late afternoon to early morning and rest during daylight hours.

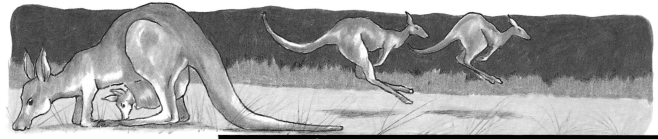

MAMMALS

COYPU (*Myocastor coypus*)

The coypu (a.k.a. the nutria) looks a lot like a large brown rat: its eyes and ears are small, its claws are sharp, and its incisor teeth are bright orange. Bright orange? That's no rat.

This semiaquatic rodent lives in marshes and on the banks of lakes and streams in southern Brazil, Bolivia, Paraguay, Uruguay, Argentina, and Chile. Although the coypu, a strict vegetarian, can get around on land, it's most at home in the water, where it browses on water plants. It has webbed hind feet to aid water locomotion.

Coypus usually breed year-round, and females produce two or three litters of one to 13 young. Newborn coypus weigh about 200 grams (about 7 ounces) and are furry and wide-eyed. Fully grown coypus may weigh in at 10 kilograms (22 pounds).

Coypus love life in the water, and they often make grassy platforms or rafts where they hang out, eat, and groom themselves.

Not only does the coypu have bright orange front teeth but those teeth never stop growing! *All* rodents have four front teeth that grow for a lifetime. These teeth are worn down by daily use. There's also a gap between tooth rows so that the rodent can gnaw with its mouth closed!

MAMMALS

AARDVARK (Orycteropus afer)

The aardvark looks a bit like a humpbacked pig. It has extremely thick skin and bristly gray hairs. Its piglike snout is whiskered, and its waxy ears can move in separate directions at the same time. The aardvark depends on its long, sticky tongue to gather termites and ants to eat. (When the aardvark's tongue is not in use, it curls up at the end like a coil spring.)

A keen sense of smell helps aarvarks sniff out termite nests and anthills, which they dig up. They also have sharp ears—the better to listen for insects on the move. A column of marching termites may stretch a distance of about 40 meters (130 feet!), and that many termites make a lot of noise.

Because it burrows, the aardvark is considered a pest—and is killed—by many farmers. But farmers have learned that when there are no aardvarks to control the termite population, termites may devour farm crops.

Aardvarks live in much of Africa. "Aardvark" is Afrikaans for "earth pig," and indeed this piglike critter is an energetic burrower.

In soft earth, aardvarks can dig quicker than several kids with shovels!

MAMMALS

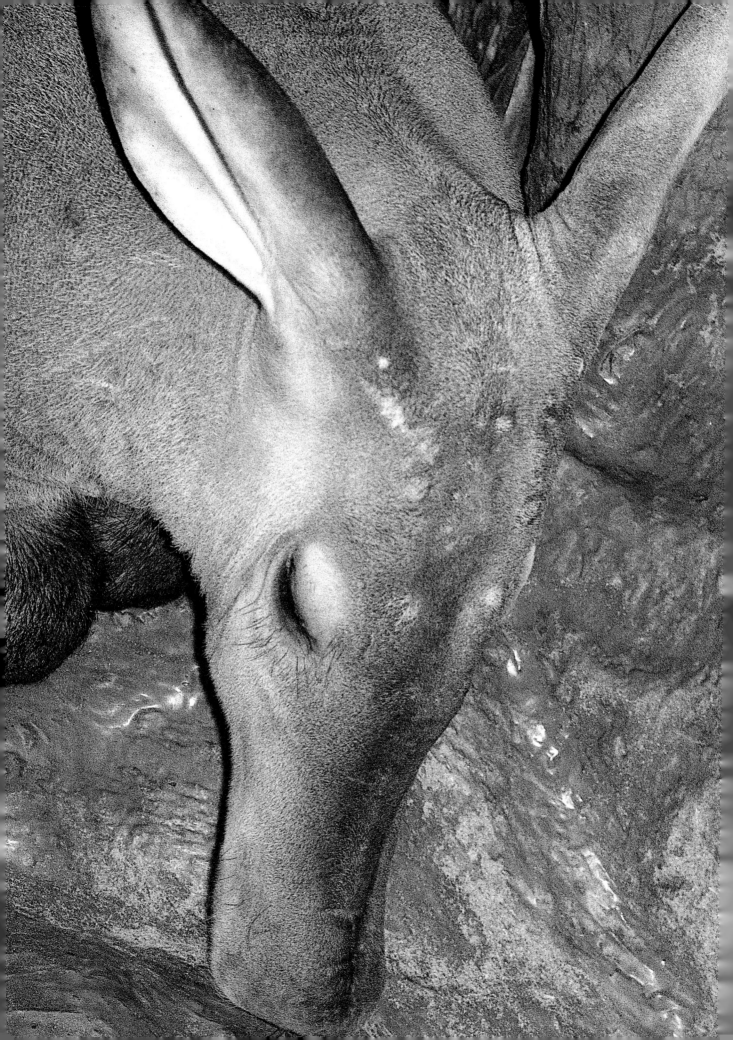

This glossarized index will help you find specific information about the mammals in this book. It will also help you understand the meaning of some of the words that are used.